The Lobster Lady

ALEXANDRA S. D. HINRICHS   *Illustrated by* JAMIE HOGAN

 Charlesbridge

The Lobster Lady wakes while the world still sleeps.

Out the window, through the darkness and across a yard, she can just make out the house where she was born, 102 years ago.

She plates the chocolate doughnuts (baked the night before), and her son, Max, prepares coffee, milky and sweet, just the way she likes it.

After breakfast she applies her lipstick. The Lobster Lady is ready. Her boat and the sea await.

"Morning, Virginia! Morning, Max!" a lobsterman greets them. They smile in turn.

On board they don oil slicks and boots and head to the co-op.

"Hello, Ginny!" men holler from the dock.

Virginia's eyes twinkle as she waves.

Once she and Max have filled their boat with gas and bait, they turn toward the rising sun.

The motor whirs as Virginia puts slippery silver pogies into salt-roughened bait bags. When they reach their first buoy, Max hauls in the traps: "Let's see what we've got!" Gulls cry as metal clangs. They're hoping for a good catch, too!

Virginia reaches inside the trap and—*careful,
caaareful!*—pulls out the first lobster. It scurries
onto the table, raising its claws for battle. Then—
careful, caaareful!—Virginia measures the lobster.
"No good!" she announces and tosses the too-small
crustacean into the sea.

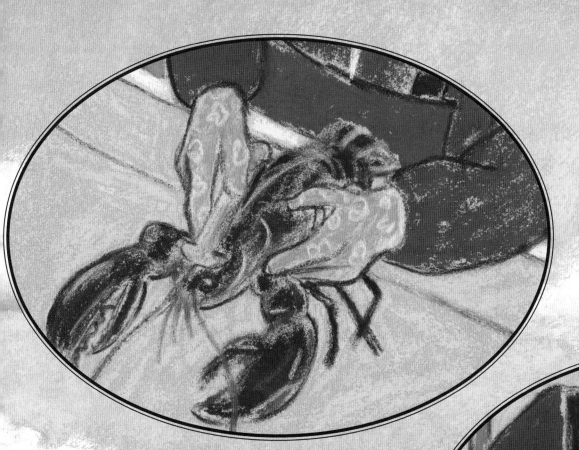

She finds eggs on the next one, so back it goes, too.

The third one measures out. She finds no eggs or marks. *Careful, caaareful!* She bands the claws, then places it in the tank.

Lobster after lobster, trap after trap, Virginia and Max work. They know the rhythms of the job so well that they don't talk much, letting the quiet loudness of the ocean and the boat wash over them.

Virginia finds a lone crab and sets it aside for her daughter's husband, thinking of his favorite meal. Before she can band it, though, it bites her with its strong claw! She drops it into a bucket, and Max steers the boat to shore. They need a doctor.

The crab got her good. Seven stitches later, the
doctor looks up at Virginia. He takes in her lipstick,
earrings, and gray curls.

"What were you doing out there, anyway?"
he chides.

Virginia pauses. She remembers . . .

. . . the island.

The smell of sawdust,
the roar of bellows,

the chatter in the store,
and the saltwater drops on her tongue.

There was always a job
for everyone. Even her.

She remembers the way her family
flowed together and apart.
The summer Saturdays crossing the bar,
cooking bean suppers,

the music and clapping and
call of the dance hall,
and her mother trying to catch her for bed.

Leaving the island and her parents behind to live in the mainland house full of aunts and her grandfather, during the long school months.

Diving into book after book,
feeling awash in the missing.
The trips to the post office, built with
the island granite that she had inside her, too.

Virginia remembers the thrill of being in charge.
Deciding to celebrate the start of summer
and her island return with too many
chocolate straws and bottles
of Moxie (that churned
in her stomach like
stormy seas).

Learning to pilot the boat—on an
ocean full of boats full of boys—
and the way the fisherman listened
when she called them to work each morning.
Hauling in her own lobster traps.

She remembers learning loss.

She remembers learning love.

And love and love
and love and love.

She remembers the years trying to find the just-right job.

The nights in the sardine factory, snipping heads and tails, that ruined her taste for herring.

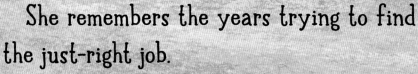

The years in the printing press office, doing whatever they needed her to do, and the day her lobsterman came home to find her hanging laundry on the line.

"I thought you went to work," he said.
"I did," she replied. "I quit. I want to go with you."
And the very next day she did.
Returning to the sea on the boat named
for her.

Now Virginia glares at the doctor.
What was she doing out there?

"I wanted to go," she answers him,
"So I did."

Back at home, Max
tells their friends and
family about the
doctor's comment.

One friend says, "You're something of a pioneer, aren't you, Ginny?"

"I'm me," Virginia responds, a glimmer of island granite in her eye.

They laugh together into the night, but not too late. . . .

The next morning, the Lobster Lady wakes
while the world still sleeps.

Her boat and the sea await.

MEET VIRGINIA

At 102 years old, Virginia Oliver is the oldest person lobstering in Maine, and maybe even in the world! She has been lobstering on and off for over ninety-three years! Fondly known as "The Lobster Lady" among locals and "Ginny" among close friends, Virginia was born on June 6, 1920 at her grandparents' house on Clarendon Street in Rockland, Maine. She spent weekends and summers on The Neck, an island off of Andrews Island, where her father ran a general store that provided supplies to fishermen and inhabitants of other nearby islands. The family slept in adjoining bedrooms above the store and maintained a smithy (or blacksmith shop), sawmill, dance hall, and three small rental houses. Anything they needed, they made or had to retrieve from mainland. Her parents wanted Virginia and her two older siblings to have a good education, so during the school year, they sent them to live with their aunts and grandfather (her grandmother died when she was very young) on Clarendon Street. Virginia and her older sister slept in the attic. They walked to school, and Virginia also walked to the library to borrow the books she loved to read.

When summer came, they went to work—and play!—on the island again. Virginia started hauling lobsters with her older brother. She first piloted a boat by herself when she was eight years old, at a time when girls and women rarely lobstered. When asked about her motivation, she says simply that she wanted to. Plus, her father was happy to have the help. He sent her out to call the men from neighboring islands to work.

A year after her mother died, seventeen-year-old Virginia married a lobsterman who lived across from her house on the mainland. They had four children, all born at home in the same house Virginia was born in. Sometimes while her aunt, a teacher, took care of her children, Virginia worked at a sardine factory. She had to snip off their heads and tails and pack them into cans. She couldn't eat sardines after that.

When her youngest child turned nine years old, she got a job at a printing office. She worked there for more than eighteen years. One day, her husband found her in the yard at home with laundry hanging all around her and commented that he thought she had gone to work that day. She told him she had gone to work and that she quit. She wanted to go lobstering with him.

The very next day, she joined him on the boat he had named after her: *Virginia*.

CHANGES AND CHALLENGES

Virginia has seen many changes in the industry and community around her: from wooden boats and lobster traps to fiberglass boats outfitted with GPS systems and wire traps. Sardines and herring were once the most common bait used for lobstering, and there were multiple sardine factories around Maine. However, their numbers declined, and they are no longer readily available.

Virginia worries about the health and sustainability of Maine's lobster population, which she says is subject to heavy fishing pressure these days. The island remains in her family, but most of the structures from her girlhood eventually went adrift during major storms.

Despite her concerns, some things remain the same. Virginia will be the first to tell you that just like when she was a girl, she's "not scared of nothing!" If she has anything to say, she'll say it. And she has no plans to stop lobstering any time soon. She is a fiercely independent, loving, lobstering woman.

VIRGINIA'S RECIPE FOR A LOBSTER ROLL

Mix together boiled, chopped lobster meat and mayonnaise to taste.

Serve on a roll of your choice. That's it. Nice and simple.

> **"If I'm going to have a lobster roll, I want lobstah!"**
>
> —Virginia

VIRGINIA'S RECIPE FOR A BEAN SUPPER

2-pound bag of yellow eye beans
3/4 cup molasses
Water

Soak the beans overnight in a large mixing bowl in enough water to cover the beans. In the morning, pour the beans, the molasses, and any water left into a bean pot or casserole dish in the oven at 315°F.

Bake them all day long (9a.m.–5p.m.), checking every three hours or so. Serve warm and enjoy!

SOURCES

The Associated Press. "At 101, This Woman From Maine Is Still Hauling Lobsters With No Plans To Stop." NPR, September 16, 2021, sec. National. https://www.npr.org/2021/09/16/1037773633/at-101-this-woman-from-maine-is-still-hauling-lobsters-with-no-plans-to-stop.

CBS News. "Maine's Oldest Lobster Trapper Has No Plans to Retire at 101." Accessed September 26, 2021. https://www.cbsnews.com/news/maines-oldest-lobster-trapper-virginia-oliver/.

Gray, Wayne, and Dale Schierholt. Conversations with the Lobster Lady. Maine Public Community Films. GEM Productions & Schierholt Pictures, 2020. https://www.pbs.org/video/conversations-with-the-lobster-lady-tmiqyk/.

Kevin, Brian. "101 and Still Lobstering, Virginia Oliver Is Bemused By Her Celebrity." Down East Magazine, November 2021. https://downeast.com/our-towns/101-and-still-lobstering-virginia-oliver-is-bemused-by-her-celebrity/.

Virginia Oliver in discussion with the author, October 13, 2021, recording held in personal collection of Alexandra Hinrichs.

Virginia Oliver, Max Oliver, and Wayne Gray in discussion with the author, July 18, 2021, recording held in personal collection of Alexandra Hinrichs.

To Virginia, who inspires so many,
capturing lobsters and hearts alike.
And to Zack, whose love of
the ocean knows no bounds.
—A. S. D. H.

To Marty and Daisy, my beloved
Barnacles who know how to live salty.
—J. H.

Published by Charlesbridge
9 Galen Street
Watertown, MA 02472
(617) 926-0329
www.charlesbridge.com

Printed in China
(hc) 10 9 8 7 6 5 4 3 2 1

Illustrations done in chalk pastel on sanded paper
Display type set in Allora by Wesley Barnes
Text type set in Halewyn by David Kerkhoff
Printed by 1010 Printing International Limited in Huizhou,
    Guangdong, China
Production supervision by Jennifer Most Delaney
Designed by Kristen Nobles

Acknowledgments

We are incredibly grateful
to Virginia and Max Oliver,
who generously shared time
and stories with us in support
of this book. We are also
thankful to filmmaker and
historian Wayne Gray for
his conversation, feedback,
and invaluable resources,
as well as to the Rockland
Historical Society.

Virginia Oliver and
Alexandra S. D. Hinrichs,
July 1, 2022.

Photo © Wayne Gray

Library of Congress Cataloging-in-Publication Data
Names: Hinrichs, Alexandra S. D., 1984- author. | Hogan, Jamie,
    illustrator.
Title: The lobster lady / Alexandra S.D. Hinrichs; illustrated by
    Jamie Hogan.
Description: Watertown, MA: Charlesbdridge, [2023] | Includes
    bibliographical references. | Audience: Ages 5-8 | Audience:
    Grades 2-3 | Summary: "At 102-years-old, Virginia Oliver,
    or 'The Lobster Lady,' is the oldest person hauling lobster in
    Maine and possibly the world; and she still remembers life as
    a little girl—working along the rocky coast, enjoying time well
    spent with family."—Provided by publisher.
Identifiers: LCCN 2022015790 (print) | LCCN 2022015791 (ebook) |
    ISBN 9781623543938 (hardcover) | ISBN 9781632893659 (ebook)
Subjects: LCSH: Oliver, Virginia, 1920—Juvenile literature. | Lobster
    fishers—Maine—Biography—Juvenile literature. | Fishing villages—
    Maine—Juvenile literature. | Maine—Biography—Juvenile literature.
Classification: LCC SH20.O45 H56 2023 (print) | LCC SH20.O45
    (ebook) | DDC 639/.54092 [B]—dc23/eng/20220808
LC record available at https://lccn.loc.gov/2022015790
LC ebook record available at https://lccn.loc.gov/2022015791